Thirty New Hymns

Thirty New Hymns

Text by Michael Forster

*Music by Adrian Vernon Fish   Edward Elgar
Richard Runciman Terry   Christopher Tambling
Charles Gounod   June Nixon   Alan Ridout   Stanley Vann
Colin Mawby   Alan Rees   Richard Lloyd   John Marsh
Malcolm Archer   Norman Warren*

Kevin Mayhew

Thirty New Hymns is available in the following editions:

1425256	Full Music Edition
1425257	Words Edition
1425258	Cassette: a recording of all thirty hymns by the City of Bristol Choir conducted by Malcolm Archer

Copies are available from your local music or christian bookshop.
In case of difficulty please contact the publisher direct by writing to:

The Sales Department
KEVIN MAYHEW LTD
Rattlesden
Bury St Edmunds
Suffolk IP30 0SZ
Phone 0449 737978   Fax 0449 737834

Please ask for our complete catalogue of outstanding Church Music.

Front cover: *Laus Veneris*, 1873-8 (detail)
by Sir Edward Coley Burne-Jones (1833-1898)
Reproduced by courtesy of the Laing Art Gallery,
Newcastle upon Tyne (Tyne and Wear Museums).

First published in Great Britain in 1992 by

KEVIN MAYHEW LTD
Rattlesden
Bury St Edmunds
Suffolk IP30 0SZ

ISBN 0 86209 280 9

© Copyright 1992 by Kevin Mayhew Ltd.

The words and music in this book are protected by copyright and may not be reproduced in any way for sale or private use without the consent of the copyright owner.

Music setting by Tricia Oliver
Cover design by Graham Johnstone
Printed and bound in Great Britain

Contents

	Hymn Number
Angels and stars	27
As we walk from pain and sorrow	26
At your feet	30
Behold and see	6
Blest are you O God, Creator	18
Christ bids us seek his face	8
Come, Holy Spirit, come!	13
Come, let us, in this holy place	1
Cry 'Freedom!'	4
From God goes forth	28
From many grains	19
From the very depths of darkness	29
Glory to God	16
God of the nations	2
Good news to the poor	5
Hail to the risen Lord	12
He is not here	24
I do not know the man	15
In the darkness of the garden	25
Into your hands	23
It is complete!	21
Jesus meets us	14
Keep watch and pray	10
Look to the rock	3
Mary, blessed teenage mother	20
O why, my God, have you forsaken me?	7
Spirit of God	22
Such a host as none can number	9
The Creed	17
The Gloria	16
The Spirit of God	5
The voice from outside	27
We believe	17
Who would believe	11

*To my mother, Cicely, and my son, Glen,
who worship with us in the Communion of Saints*

Foreword

My initial excursion into hymn-writing had an ecumenical purpose: to offer one of the great traditional texts of the Church – the Gloria – in a form which would be more readily accessible to congregations unaccustomed to set prayers. That ecumenical factor remained an important consideration as my interest in hymn-writing developed. Whatever we are trying to do in worship, it is much better done together. Since we are now able, thankfully, to talk about what divides us, how much more should we get together to sing of those things which unite us!

Hymns enable us to do many things: to express something of the glory, the grace, the love, the power and the mystery of God, and to bring to him the successes, the failures, the celebrations and the bereavements which are our lives. This, in a nutshell, is what these hymns attempt to do – to whatever limited extent any human words can. They may be used to express praise, commitment, penitence; as credal statements, or to stimulate the imagination. I hope they may bring fresh insight into some of the great stories and images of the faith, or simply express wonder at the eternal Mystery which surrounds, infuses and embraces the universe.

An index of uses is provided for easy reference, but this is really only a guide. Users are sure to find other and better applications. And, in any case, the incarnation, passion and resurrection are, like Christ himself, ever-present realities. Christians celebrate the whole of the gospel for the whole of the year; festivals highlight particular aspects, rather than exclude all others.

I hope that congregations will find these hymns as stimulating and enjoyable to sing as I have to write.

I am grateful to many people for help and encouragement, but especially to: the various gifted composers who have provided such singable tunes; Barry Ferguson, Organist and Master of the Choristers at Rochester Cathedral, for his invaluable help in refining the texts; the people of Buckminster Road Baptist Church in Leicester, whose worship has provided the proving-ground for many of the hymns; and Jean, my wife, my critic and my friend.

MICHAEL FORSTER

1 COME, LET US, IN THIS HOLY PLACE

Text: Michael Forster   Music: Adrian Vernon Fish

Aasiaat C. M.

© Copyright 1992 Kevin Mayhew Ltd.
It is illegal to photocopy music

2 GOD OF THE NATIONS

Text: Michael Forster   Music: Edward Elgar, adapted by Alan Ridout

Malvern 8888.8

1. God of the nations, hear our prayer;
2. Father, forgive the nations' rage:
3. Here may we glorify our dead,
4. Teach us to turn our bombs to bread;
5. God of the nations, hear our prayer;

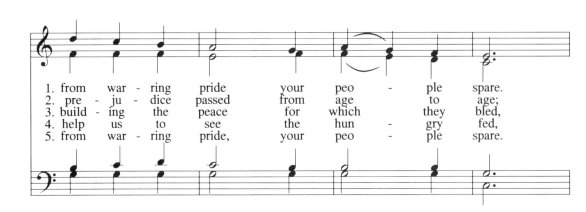

1. from warring pride your people spare.
2. prejudice passed from age to age;
3. building the peace for which they bled,
4. help us to see the hungry fed,
5. from warring pride, your people spare.

1. Let us in love and truth unite,
2. banners made sacred, life made cheap;
3. never to make their dying vain,
4. welcome the homeless, heal the lame,
5. Let us in love and truth unite,

© Copyright 1992 Kevin Mayhew Ltd.
It is illegal to photocopy music

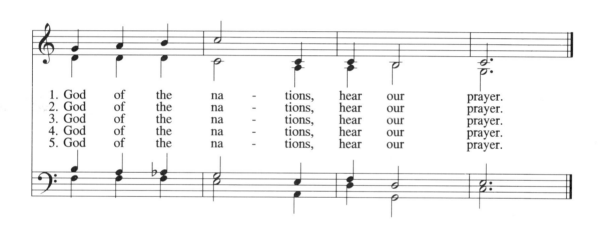

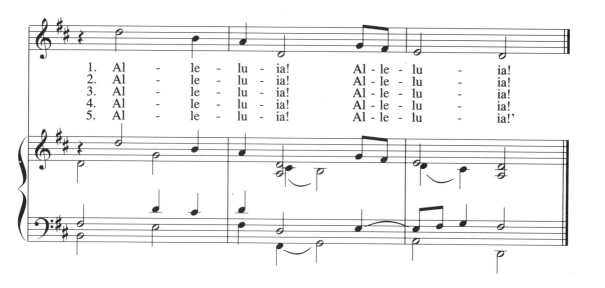

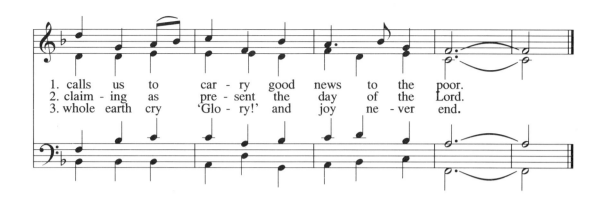

15

7 O WHY, MY GOD, HAVE YOU FORSAKEN ME?

Text: Michael Forster   Music: (based on the plainsong 'Salve mater') Colin Mawby

Vaux 10.10.10.10.10.10.

© Copyright 1992 Kevin Mayhew Ltd.
It is illegal to photocopy music

8 CHRIST BIDS US SEEK HIS FACE

Text: Michael Forster   Music: Stanley Vann

Yarwell 66.66.88

1. Christ bids us seek his face where human need is
2. When hungry people call for justice and for
3. He comes in stranger's guise; no fixed abode has
4. Where prison bars enclose in dark and lonely
5. Cold in his nakedness, to those with eyes to
6. O such mysterious grace turns water into

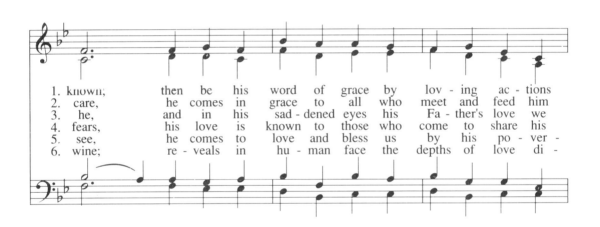

1. known; then be his word of grace by loving actions
2. care, he comes in grace to all who meet and feed him
3. he, and in his sad-dened eyes his Father's love we
4. fears, his love is known to those who come to share his
5. see, he comes to love and bless us by his pover-
6. wine; reveals in human face the depths of love di-

1. shown. In sin and shame, undignified, the
2. there; and judgement speaks to those with power, who
3. see. But O the shame the wealth we miss when
4. tears. But foolish sin when, passing by, we
5. ty. But sad the one who lets him freeze, and
6. vine! Here Myst'ry find: his form, revealed yet

© Copyright 1992 Kevin Mayhew Ltd.
It is illegal to photocopy music

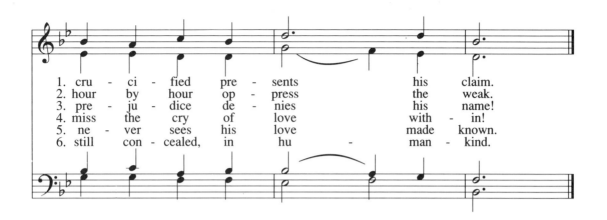

10 KEEP WATCH AND PRAY

Text: Michael Forster   Music: John Marsh

Redcliffe 11.10.11.10

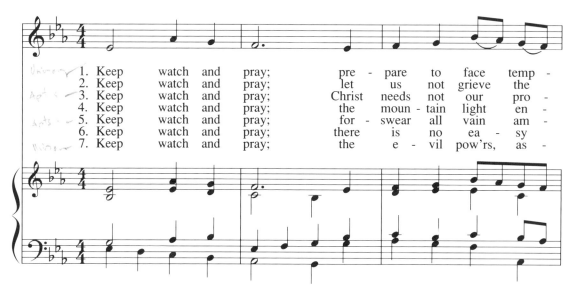

1. Keep watch and pray; pre-pare to face temp-
2. Keep watch and pray; let us not grieve the
3. Keep watch and pray; Christ needs not our pro-
4. Keep watch and pray; the moun-tain light en-
5. Keep watch and pray; for-swear all vain am-
6. Keep watch and pray; there is no ea-sy
7. Keep watch and pray; the e-vil pow'rs, as-

1. ta - tion. Let us not seek to
2. Spi - rit, por - tray-ing true as
3. tec - tion our good in - ten - tions
4. thrals us! Here would we stay, a-
5. bi - tion; in God's good time his
6. glo - ry how pre - ma - ture that
7. cen - dant, with all their might, con-

© Copyright 1992 Kevin Mayhew Ltd.
It is illegal to photocopy music

11 WHO WOULD BELIEVE

Text: Michael Forster   Music: Malcolm Archer

Hurst L.M.

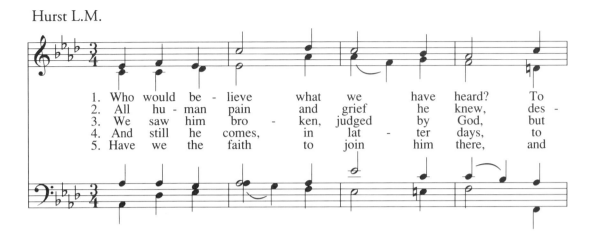

1. Who would believe what we have heard? To
2. All human pain and grief he knew, des-
3. We saw him broken, judged by God, but
4. And still he comes, in latter days, to
5. Have we the faith to join him there, and

1. whom has God revealed his might?
2. pised and cruelly cast aside;
3. ours the sins that made him bleed;
4. judge the strong and shame the wise,
5. feel the sharpness of his pain;

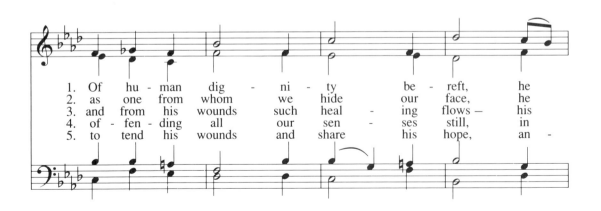

1. Of human dignity bereft, he
2. as one from whom we hide our face, he
3. and from his wounds such healing flows — his
4. of-fending all our senses still, in
5. to tend his wounds and share his hope, an-

© Copyright 1992 Kevin Mayhew Ltd.
It is illegal to photocopy music

1. was of - fen - sive to our sight.
2. stood a - mong the vi - li - fied.
3. grief has met our deep - est need!
4. count - less an - guished hu - man eyes.
5. nounc - ing love's e - ter - nal reign?

12 HAIL TO THE RISEN LORD

Text: Michael Forster   Music: Christopher Tambling

Roberts D.S.M.

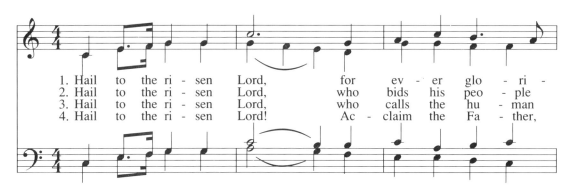

1. Hail to the risen Lord, for ever glorified, presenting at the Father's throne his wounded limbs and side. Behold, the triune
2. Hail to the risen Lord, who bids his people rise from sin that human souls enslaves and persons' worth denies, to seek the Father's
3. Hail to the risen Lord, who calls the human race, above the party line, to seek the politics of grace: the love that will not
4. Hail to the risen Lord! Acclaim the Father, Son and Spirit, by whose power alone the many can be one. O all embracing

© Copyright 1992 Kevin Mayhew Ltd.
It is illegal to photocopy music

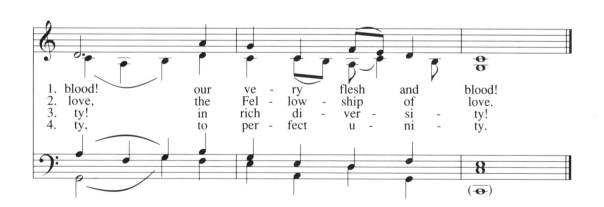

13 COME, HOLY SPIRIT, COME!

Text: Michael Forster   Music: Colin Mawby

Donnybrook D.S.M.

1. Come, Holy Spirit, come! inflame our souls with
2. All knowing Spirit, prove the poverty of
3. Come with the gift to *heal* the wounds of guilt and
4. Spirit of truth, arise; inspire the *prophet's*
5. Give us the *tongues* to speak, in every time and
6. Come, Holy Spirit, dance within our hearts to-

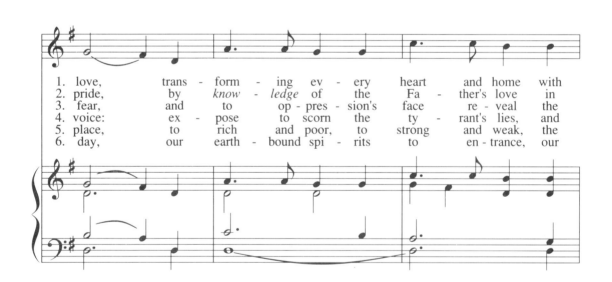

1. love, transforming every heart and home with
2. pride, by *knowledge* of the Father's love in
3. fear, and to oppression's face reveal the
4. voice: expose to scorn the tyrant's lies, and
5. place, to rich and poor, to strong and weak, the
6. day, our earth-bound spirits to entrance, our

© Copyright 1992 Kevin Mayhew Ltd.
It is illegal to photocopy music

14 JESUS MEETS US

Text: Michael Forster   Music: Adrian Vernon Fish

Frederiksen 87.87

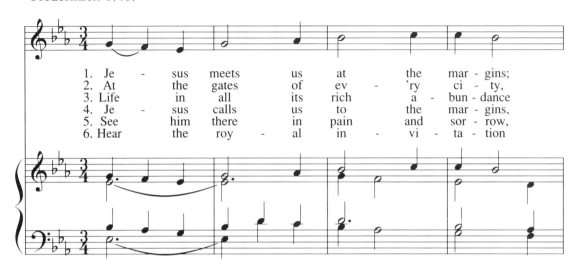

1. Je - sus meets us at the mar - gins;
2. At the gates of ev - 'ry ci - ty,
3. Life in all its rich a - bun - dance
4. Je - sus calls us to the mar - gins,
5. See him there in pain and sor - row,
6. Hear the roy - al in - vi - ta - tion

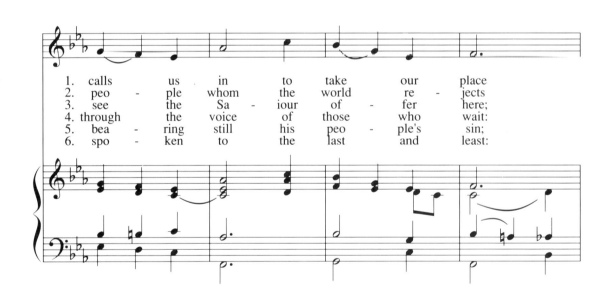

1. calls us in to take our place
2. peo - ple whom the world re - jects
3. see the Sa - viour of - fer here;
4. through the voice of those who wait:
5. bea - ring still his peo - ple's sin;
6. spo - ken to the last and least:

© Copyright 1992 Kevin Mayhew Ltd.
It is illegal to photocopy music

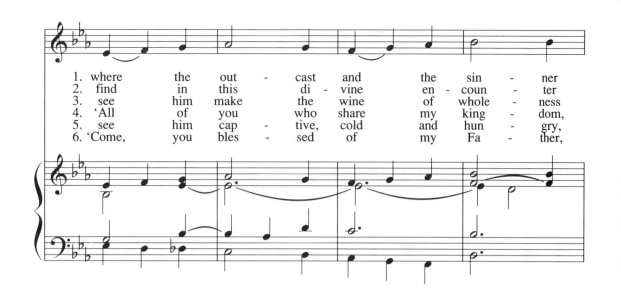

15 I DO NOT KNOW THE MAN
Text: Michael Forster   Music: Richard Lloyd

© Copyright 1992 Kevin Mayhew Ltd.
It is illegal to photocopy music

16 THE GLORIA

Text: Michael Forster   Music: Stanley Vann

© Copyright 1992 Kevin Mayhew Ltd.
It is illegal to photocopy music

17 THE CREED

Text: Michael Forster   Music: Colin Mawby

Wentstown 87.87.87

1. We be-lieve in one al-migh-ty God and Fa-ther
2. We be-lieve in one Re-deem-er, Christ, the Fa-ther's
3. All for us and our sal-va-tion, Christ his glo-ry
4. He has burst the grave a-sun-der, ri-sing as the
5. We ac-claim the Ho-ly Spi-rit, of all life the
6. Ho-ly church, and u-ni-ver-sal, a-pos-to-lic

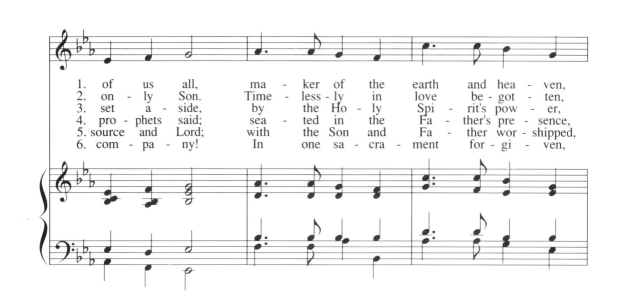

1. of us all, ma-ker of the earth and hea-ven,
2. on-ly Son. Time-less-ly in love be-got-ten,
3. set a-side, by the Ho-ly Spi-rit's pow-er,
4. pro-phets said; sea-ted in the Fa-ther's pre-sence,
5. source and Lord; with the Son and Fa-ther wor-shipped,
6. com-pa-ny! In one sa-cra-ment for-gi-ven,

© Copyright 1992 Kevin Mayhew Ltd.
It is illegal to photocopy music

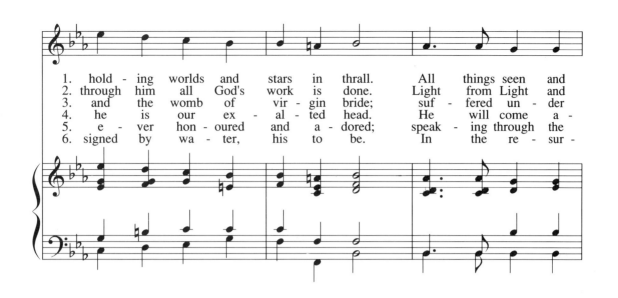
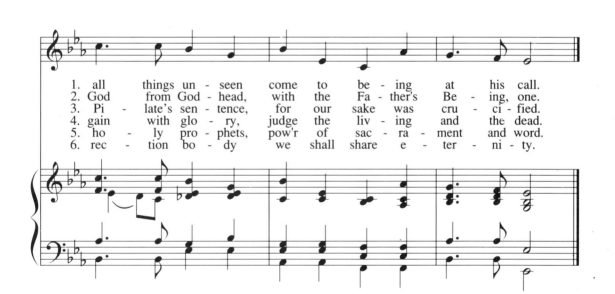

18 BLEST ARE YOU O GOD, CREATOR

Text: Michael Forster   Music: June Nixon

Castlemaine 87.87.D

1. Blest are you, O God, Creator; through your
2. Blest are you, O God, Creator; by your
3. Blest are you, O God, Creator: Light of

1. goodness, bread we share, by the earth con-
2. grace we offer wine, work of human
3. lights and Power of powers, yet in humble

1. ceived and given, made by human skill and
2. hands combining with the goodness of the
3. love accepting gifts from hands as poor as

© Copyright 1992 Kevin Mayhew Ltd.
It is illegal to photocopy music

20 MARY, BLESSED TEENAGE MOTHER

Text: Michael Forster   Music: Alan Ridout

Black Madonna 87.87.77

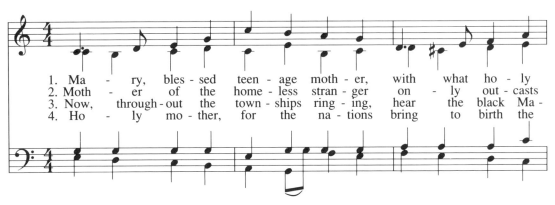
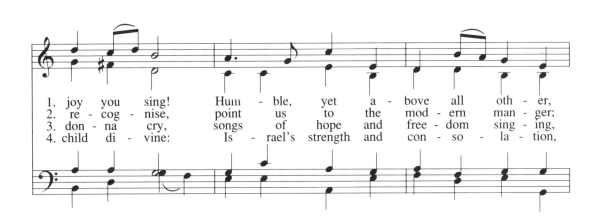
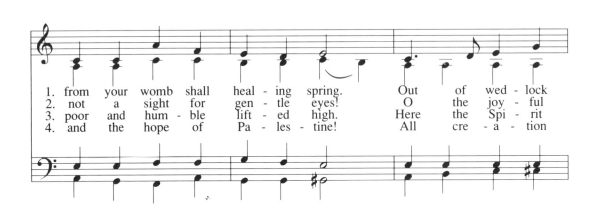

© Copyright 1992 Kevin Mayhew Ltd.
It is illegal to photocopy music

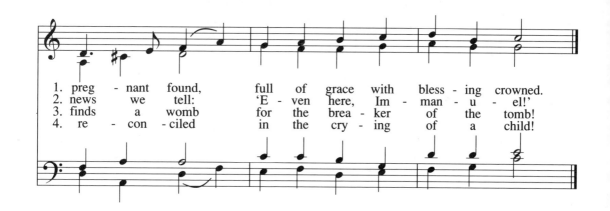

1. preg - nant found, full of grace with bless - ing crowned.
2. news we tell: 'E - ven here, Im - man - u - el!'
3. finds a womb for the brea - ker of the tomb!
4. re - con - ciled in the cry - ing of a child!

21 IT IS COMPLETE!

Text: Michael Forster   Music: Alan Rees

Emmaus 10.10.10.10

1. 'It is complete!' The cry of triumph rings;
   love conquers all, enduring to the death;
   in human frailty, never more divine,

2. 'It is complete!' No compromise he makes
   for pain and death cannot his voice suppress,
   nor turn his lips to harsh and spiteful words,

3. 'It is complete!' He shows the power of grace:
   opens new realms of possibility;
   calls us to share the victory of love,

4. 'It is complete!' let all creation cry,
   when into ploughshares all our swords we beat;
   when peace and justice, like a river, flow,

© Copyright 1992 Kevin Mayhew Ltd.
It is illegal to photocopy music

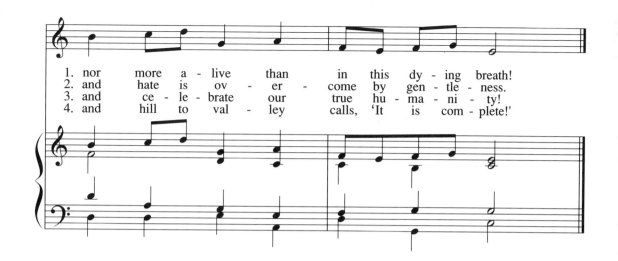

22 SPIRIT OF GOD

Text: Michael Forster Music: Charles Gounod adapted and arranged by Alan Ridout

Spirit of God DLM

1. Spirit of God, O set us free; let no dark fears our souls confine. Lead us by new, uncharted ways; unfold the Mystery divine. We long to see, to touch, to know, and fear the risk that faith demands; O help us
2. Spirit of God, the breath of life, give strength to hearts and limbs that tire; lead us through mysteries untold, make truth and freedom our desire. You call us on to life and hope from all that would our souls enslave; O may our
3. Spirit of God, come like a fire to lift our spirits in the night; burn in the coldness of our hearts, and lead us on toward the light. And when, with mem'ry's distant view, we long for some enchanted past, then give us

© Copyright 1992 Kevin Mayhew Ltd.
It is illegal to photocopy music

23 INTO YOUR HANDS

Text: Michael Forster   Music: John Marsh

Ravenhill 76.76.D

1. 'Into your hands, O Father, my spirit I commend,'
the words of one so faithful, who trusted to the end.
His dying thus completed the path of life he trod,
in

2. From birth to death consistent, rejecting earthly fame;
in perfect trust obeying the one from whom he came,
he chose to be included with those the world denied:
the

© Copyright 1992 Kevin Mayhew Ltd.
It is illegal to photocopy music

1. faith-ful trust pur-su-ing the pur-po-ses of God.
2. bro-ken and the guil-ty with whom he lived and died.

See over for verse 3

25 IN THE DARKNESS OF THE GARDEN

Text: Michael Forster Music: Colin Mawby

Rathmines 87.87.87.87.D

1. In the darkness of the garden, see the tears and bloody sweat; such a bitter preparation for a darkness deeper yet. What a dreadful test he faces; hear his agonising plea: 'If it

2. In the sorrow of the garden, see the friends who fall away. They who promised love undying cannot stay awake to pray. We, with them, must hear him asking, less in anger than in pain, 'Such a

3. In the silence of the garden, feel the chill and leaden air; hear the dark abyss resounding with the great unanswered prayer! Yet, in that dread desolation, he is still his Father's Son, by the

© Copyright 1992 Kevin Mayhew Ltd.
It is illegal to photocopy music

26 AS WE WALK FROM PAIN AND SORROW

Text: Michael Forster Music: Christopher Tambling

Aichison's 8.7.8.7.D

© Copyright 1992 Kevin Mayhew Ltd.
It is illegal to photocopy music

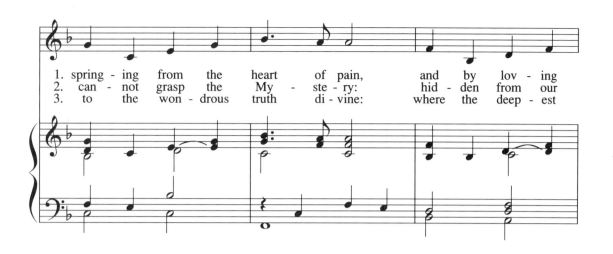
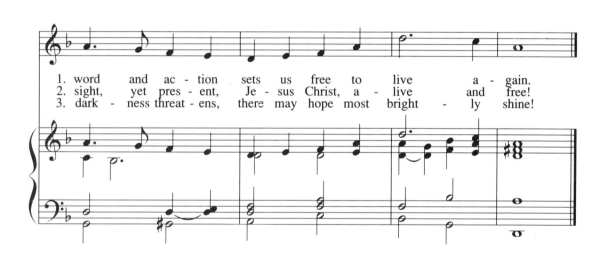

27 THE VOICE FROM OUTSIDE

Text: Michael Forster   Music: Alan Ridout

Saint Monica 10.10.10.10

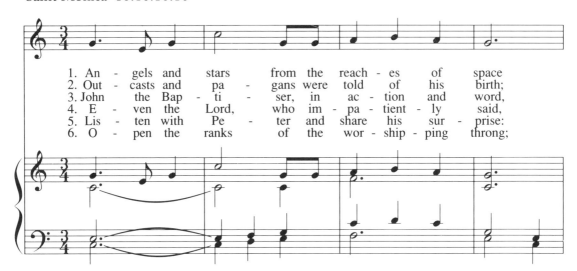

1. Angels and stars from the reaches of space
2. Outcasts and pagans were told of his birth;
3. John the Baptiser, in action and word,
4. Even the Lord, who impatiently said,
5. Listen with Peter and share his surprise:
6. Open the ranks of the worshipping throng;

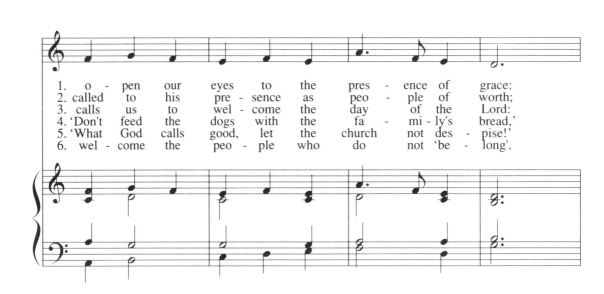

1. open our eyes to the presence of grace:
2. called to his presence as people of worth;
3. calls us to welcome the day of the Lord:
4. 'Don't feed the dogs with the family's bread,'
5. 'What God calls good, let the church not despise!'
6. welcome the people who do not 'belong'.

© Copyright 1992 Kevin Mayhew Ltd.
It is illegal to photocopy music

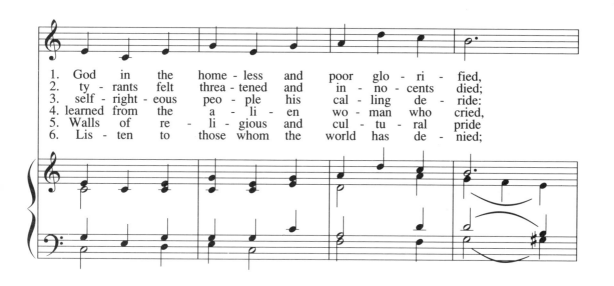

1. God in the home-less and poor glo-ri-fied,
2. ty-rants felt threa-tened and in-no-cents died;
3. self-right-eous peo-ple his cal-ling de-ride:
4. learned from the a-li-en wo-man who cried,
5. Walls of re-li-gious and cul-tu-ral pride
6. Lis-ten to those whom the world has de-nied;

1. speak-ing a-new with the voice from out-side.
2. such is the fear of the voice from out-side.
3. 'What is your claim?' 'I'm the voice from out-side!'
4. 'Lis-ten, O Lord, to the voice from out-side!'
5. crum-ble to dust at the voice from out-side.
6. Chris-tians, a-wake to the voice from out-side!

28 FROM GOD GOES FORTH

Text: Michael Forster   Music: Richard Lloyd

Stalling Busk D.L.M.

1. From God goes forth the light of truth: his judgement all the world shall see; in places dark with death's despair, his word is life and liberty. When
2. His piercing light, with fiery probe, can penetrate the prison wall; so guilty fear gives way to hope, as deathless love transfigures all. And
3. The messenger proclaims the word: 'Prepare the way, the Lord is near.' The one on whom the nations call within his temple will appear. Where
4. Among the peoples of the earth, the Lord of hosts will take his place, to make the poor abode his home and simple food a means of grace. His
5. Compassion bids us face the dark, and faith's discernment brings to sight the presence of the God of hope in inextinguishable light. So

© Copyright 1992 Kevin Mayhew Ltd.
It is illegal to photocopy music

29 FROM THE VERY DEPTHS OF DARKNESS

Text: Michael Forster   Music: Christopher Tambling

Cameron's 15.15.15.4 with refrain

1. From the very depths of darkness springs a bright and living light; out of falsehood and deceit a greater truth is brought to sight; in the halls of death, defiant, Life is
2. Jesus meets us at the dawning of the resurrection day; speaks our name with love, and gently says that here we may not stay: 'Do not cling to me, but go to all the
3. So proclaim it in the high-rise, in the hostel let it ring; make it known in Cardboard City, let the homeless rise and sing: 'He is Lord of life abundant, and he
4. In the heartlands of oppression, sound the cry of liberty: where the poor are crucified, behold the Lord of Calvary; from the fear of death and dying, Christ has
5. To the tyrant, tell the gospel of a love he's never known in his guarded palace-tomb, condemned to live and die alone: 'Take the risk of love and freedom; Christ has
6. When our spirits are entombed in mortal prejudice and pride; when the gates of hell itself are firmly bolted from inside; at the bidding of his Spirit, we may

© Copyright 1992 Kevin Mayhew Ltd.
It is illegal to photocopy music

30 AT YOUR FEET

Text: Michael Forster   Music: Alan Rees

Sacrum Convivium 87. 87. 87

1. At your feet, great God, we offer bread, the sign of hope we share; all the fullness of creation in the feast that you prepare. Christ our host, in risen splendour, gives us food beyond compare.

2. Now, in humble adoration, drawn by grace, we offer here wine that speaks of love's oblation, life from death and hope from fear. Sharing in his cup of sorrow, our Redeemer we revere.

3. Here, most holy God, we offer, with the saints in full accord, hearts and gifts for your acceptance, broken dreams to be restored. All creation cries for healing; you alone such grace afford!

© Copyright 1992 Kevin Mayhew Ltd.
It is illegal to photocopy music

Notes on Some of the Hymns

1 *Come, let us, in this holy place*
(Micah 4: 2-4) and
2 *God of the nations*
These two hymns are particularly suitable for Remembrance Sunday. But they need not be restricted to that, and are open to use in a variety of ways in normal weekly worship.

4 *Cry 'Freedom!'*
This hymn is a response to the Presidential Address at the 1991 Baptist Assembly, on the theme *Cry 'Freedom!'*. There are of course many ways of being 'un-free'. Apart from the obvious examples of oppression to be seen around the world, there are the subtler forms which we all encounter. In some christian congregations people are enslaved by dogma. Discouraged from voicing sincere questions, they are not free to make the journey of faith, into the great mystery that is God. In a more general sense, all of us are slaves to something, and need to be helped to move from self-centredness to the true freedom of living for each other.

6 *Behold and See*
(See notes under 11 *Who would believe*)

7 *O why, my God, have you forsaken me?*
The trinitarian experience of the crucifixion has been described in terms of a bereft Father and a forsaken Son, in a broken Spirit of fellowship. This helpful image gives us an opening into the eternal mystery of the passion, for only if this brokenness penetrated right to the heart of the trinitarian relationships can God in any real sense be said to have 'experienced death'. This hymn attempts to explore that concept, and highlight the healing power of shared brokenness.

9 *Such a host as none can number*
(Revelation 7:9-17)
God is the same yesterday, today and forever. So the God who desires a perfect creation in the future, presumably would not object to having it now! The vision of the future kingdom, far from anaesthetising us to the inhumanity of the present, should protest loudly against it.

10 *Keep watch and pray*
This hymn was used similarly to *From God goes forth* (28), but in Lent – as part of a Lent Vigil, based on the temptations of Christ. Those temptations are still presented to the Church today, and are reflected in the Bible passages cited. Verse one was sung on Lent One; verses one and two on Lent Two, and so on, until the whole hymn was sung on Good Friday.

The biblical references for each verse are:
1 Lent 1: Luke 4:1-13
           Jesus is tempted to abuse his power
2 Lent 2: Matthew 12:22-32
           The pharisees slander Jesus
3 Lent 3: Matthew 16:13-end
           Peter obstructs Jesus
4 Lent 4: Matthew 17:1-13
           The Transfiguration
5 Lent 5: Mark 10:32-45
           The desire for status
6 Palm Sunday Matthew 21:1-13
           The fickle crowd
7 Good Friday John 19:1-37

11 *Who would believe* (Isaiah 53:1-5)
6 *Behold and see* (Isaiah 42:1-4)
These two hymns are based on the Servant Songs. It is too easy to see these passages simply with the hindsight of the gospel. Rather, the imagery should speak freely – as it originally did – of events and situations of our own day. The question is

not only, 'Who is the servant?' but, 'Where do *we* fit into these images?' It is not a comfortable question.

12 *Hail to the risen Lord*
Without making any assumptions at the literal level, the story of the bodily ascension of Christ, seen in the light of the doctrine of the Trinity, makes a powerful statement about the divine/human relationship, and deals a fatal blow to the neo-Platonic dualism which has so degraded humanity and perverted the christian gospel.

13 *Come, Holy Spirit, come!*
(I Corinthians 12:8-11; I Corinthians 13)
Too often, the gifts of the Spirit are assumed to be for the private gratification of the Church. This seems to me totally against biblical principles. The gift of tongues is a prime example, having been given to break down barriers and enable communication. Of course we are right to pray for the gifts of the Spirit, but with the needs of others in mind.

14 *Jesus meets us at the margins*
In the Bible, many important encounters take place at the gate, with a clear image of the marginalised being met at the edge of society and enabled to find a place at the centre. Here we own and celebrate that experience. But the twist is, of course, that once that has happened, we become those on the inside, and are called to return to the gate, to meet . . . Whom?

16 *The Gloria*
17 *The Creed*
Here, the Gloria and the Nicene Creed are offered in the form of hymns. Apart from offering these beautiful traditional texts in a fresh form, it is also hoped that these settings will enable people from different liturgical traditions to worship together.

18 *Blest are you, O God, Creator*
19 *From many grains*
30 *At your feet*
These three eucharistic hymns may be sung simply as hymns, but their effectiveness is greater if used in the way they were intended – i.e. at the end of an offertory procession. A loaf of bread, a chalice of wine, and the gifts of the congregation are presented in the respective verses and elevated by the minister into full view of the congregation.

The first hymn of the three is based on the traditional Jewish graces used in some church traditions. Another way of using this particular one would be to sing just the first two verses, separately, at the distribution of the bread and wine, where the liturgical practice permits.

20 *Mary, blessed teenage mother*
The image of birth is a powerful one in the Bible, suggesting the painful bringing about of a new creation. At Christmas, we celebrate this in the story of a young, homeless woman pushed aside by society, painfully bringing to birth the hope of the world. She does not allow us to consign her to the past, but cries out to us to recognise her, and her child, in the apparent hopelessness of the present.

From the mangers of our present society, wherever hope struggles to emerge in the midst of oppression, we hear the cries of the Madonna and her child. They are black, they are white: they are Israeli and they are Palestinian; they are Roman Catholic and they are Protestant. And they are everywhere. Thank God!

22 *Spirit of God*
It is natural to seek for certainty and security, but faith entails a willingness to move on; sometimes actually to leave what seems certain and step into the unknown. The people of Israel found the 'certainty'

of Egypt easier to handle than the journey of faith. So, today we may hear the Spirit calling us to leave behind the certainties of dogma and take the risk of being open to new and exciting truth.

24 *He is not here*
'He is not here – he is risen. Why do you seek the living among the dead?'
The church has many written documents: creeds and dogmas, liturgies and hymns, and most of all the Bible itself. All of these bear powerful witness to the resurrection. Like the tomb, however, they cannot contain Christ, and the voice from within them sends us out to seek his living presence in the compelling, ever new realities of life.

25 *In the darkness of the garden*
The 'dark night of the soul' is not an invention of the mystics, but a human reality. In the agony of Gethsemane, Jesus' prayer is met by a dreadful silence. This is the experience of countless christians down the centuries, and the gospel is that, even in the depths of such Godforsakenness, faith is still possible. Indeed, it is there that it finds its deepest meaning and fulfilment.

26 *As we walk from pain and sorrow*
(Luke 24:13-35)
The Emmaus Road is part of our common experience. All of us, at some time, will need to retreat for a while from a place of pain, and we hope that there will be an Emmaus to which we can go. We may also hope that some encounter will take place which will enable us to return to 'Jerusalem' and find that the place of pain becomes, by grace, the birthplace of hope.

However, for many people – in some cases whole communities and nations – Emmaus does not seem to be there. It is appropriate to ask ourselves whether God is calling the Church to become that for them.

27 *The voice from outside*
The voice from outside announces, challenges, sometimes threatens. Even Jesus, in his encounter with the Syro-Phoenician woman, had his understanding of mission broadened by it. (Mark 7:27-30)

28 *From God goes forth*
Advent celebrates the coming of God into the world, as light shining in the darkness. If we look into the dark places of our own society, we shall find Christ already there, and calling us to join him so that the light can shine more brightly.

This hymn originally accompanied a series of Advent Candle Ceremonies which attempted to do just that. Verse one was sung on Advent One, verses one and two on Advent Two, and so on until the whole hymn was sung on Christmas Day. There is, of course, no reason why it may not be sung as a straightforward hymn.

30 *At you feet*
(See 18 *Blest are you, O God, Creator*)

Index of Uses

GOD

THE FATHER

Blest are you O God, Creator	18
Come let us, in this holy place	1
From God goes forth	28
Glory to God	16
God of the nations	2
Into your hands	23
O why, my God, have you forsaken me?	7
Such a host as none can number	9
The Creed	17
The Gloria	16
We believe	17

THE SON

Angels and stars	27
As we walk from pain and sorrow	26
Christ bids us seek his face	8
From God goes forth	28
From the very depths of darkness	29
Glory to God	16
Hail to the risen Lord	12
He is not here	24
I do not know the man	15
In the darkness of the garden	25
Into your hands	23
It is complete!	21
Jesus meets us	14
Keep watch and pray	10
Mary, blessed teenage mother	20
O why, my God, have you forsaken me?	7
Such a host as none can number	9
The Creed	17
The Gloria	16
The voice from outside	27
We believe	17

THE HOLY SPIRIT

Angels and stars	27
Come, Holy Spirit, come!	13
From many grains	19
Good news to the poor	5
Hail to the risen Lord	12
In the darkness of the garden	25
Keep watch and pray	10
Mary, blessed teenage mother	20
O why, my God, have you forsaken me	7
Spirit of God	22
The Spirit of God	5
The Creed	17
The voice from outside	27
We believe	17

THE TRINITY

Come, Holy Spirit, come!	13
Glory to God	16
Hail to the risen Lord	12
In the darkness of the garden	25
O why, my God, have you forsaken me	7
We believe	17
The Creed	17
The Gloria	16

THE GOSPEL

COMMITMENT

Christ bids us seek his face	8
Come, Holy Spirit, come!	13
Cry 'Freedom!'	4
From God goes forth	28
From the very depths of darkness	29
God of the nations	2
Good news to the poor	5
He is not here	24
I do not know the man	15
In the darkness of the garden	25
Into your hands	23
It is complete!	21
Jesus meets us	14
Keep watch and pray	10
Look to the rock	3
Such a host as none can number	9
The Spirit of God	5

FAITH

As we walk from pain and sorrow	26
Behold and see	6
Christ bids us seek his face	8
Come, Holy Spirit, come!	13
From God goes forth	28
From the very depths of darkness	29
He is not here	24
In the darkness of the garden	25
Into your hands	23
It is complete!	21
Keep watch and pray	10
Look to the rock	3
Mary, blessed teenage mother	20
O why, my God, have you forsaken me?	7
Spirit of God	22
Such a host as none can number	9
The Creed	17
We believe	17
Who would believe	11

FORGIVENESS

At your feet	30
Blest are you, O God, Creator	18
From God goes forth	28
From many grains	19
Good news to the poor	5
Hail to the risen Lord	12
I do not know the man	15
It is complete!	21
Jesus meets us	14
Mary, blessed teenage mother	20
O why, my God, have you forsaken me?	7
Such a host as none can number	9
The Spirit of God	5
We believe	17
Who would believe	11

GRACE

Angels and stars	27
As we walk from pain and sorrow	26
At your feet	30
Blest are you O God, Creator	18
Come, Holy Spirit, come!	13
From God goes forth	28
From many grains	19
Good news to the poor	5
Hail to the risen Lord	12
He is not here	24
In the darkness of the garden	25
It is complete!	21
Jesus meets us	14
Look to the rock	3
Mary, blessed teenage mother	20
Spirit of God	22
Such a host as none can number	9
The Creed	17
The Spirit of God	5
The voice from outside	27
We believe	17

HEALING

As we walk from pain and sorrow	26
Behold and see	6
Christ bids us seek his face	8
Come, Holy Spirit, come!	13
From God goes forth	28
God of the nations	2
Good news to the poor	5
Mary, blessed teenage mother	20
O why, my God, have you forsaken me?	7
Such a host as none can number	9
The Spirit of God	5
The Creed	17
Who would believe	11

HOPE

As we walk from pain and sorrow	26
Behold and see	6
Come, let us, in this holy place	1
From God goes forth	28
From the very depths of darkness	29
God of the nations	2
Good news to the poor	5
He is not here	24
Look to the rock	3
Mary, blessed teenage mother	20
O why, my God, have you forsaken me?	7
Spirit of God	22
Such a host as none can number	9
The Creed	17
The Spirit of God	5

We believe	17

JUSTICE AND PEACE

Angels and stars	27
Behold and see	6
Christ bids us seek his face	8
Come, Holy Spirit, come!	13
Come, let us, in this holy place	1
Cry 'Freedom!'	4
From God goes forth	28
From many grains	19
From the very depths of darkness	29
God of the nations	2
Good news to the poor	5
Hail to the risen Lord	12
He is not here	24
Into your hands	23
It is complete!	21
Jesus meets us	14
Mary, blessed teenage mother	20
Such a host as none can number	9
The Spirit of God	5
The voice from outside	27
Who would believe	11

LOVE

As we walk from pain and sorrow	26
Behold and see	6
Come, let us, in this holy place	1
From God goes forth	28
From the very depths of darkness	29
God of the nations	2
Good news to the poor	5
He is not here	24
Look to the rock	3
Mary, blessed teenage mother	20
O why, my God, have you forsaken me?	7
Spirit of God	22
Such a host as none can number	9
The Creed	17
The Spirit of God	5
We believe	17

REDEMPTION

As we walk from pain and sorrow	26
At your feet	30
Behold and see	6
Blest are you O God, Creator	18
Come, Holy Spirit, come!	13
Come, let us, in this holy place	1
Cry 'Freedom!'	4
From God goes forth	28
From many grains	19
From the very depths of darkness	29
Glory to God	16
God of the nations	2
Good news to the poor	5
Hail to the risen Lord	12
I do not know the man	15
It is complete!	21
Jesus meets us	14
Look to the rock	3
Mary, blessed teenage mother	20
O why, my God, have you forsaken me?	7
Such a host as none can number	9
The Creed	17
The Gloria	16
The Spirit of God	5
We believe	17
Who would believe	11

THE CHURCH: THE PEOPLE OF GOD

THE COMMUNION OF SAINTS

At your feet	30
Blest are you O God, Creator	18
Come, let us, in this holy place	1
From many grains	19
God of the nations	2
Hail to the risen Lord	12
Look to the rock	3
Mary, blessed teenage mother	20
Such a host as none can number	9
The Creed	17
We believe	17

MARY

Mary, blessed teenage mother	20
The Creed	17
We believe	17

THE SERVING COMMUNITY

Angels and stars	27
At your feet	30
Behold and see	6
Blest are you O God, Creator	18
Christ bids us seek his face	8
Come, Holy Spirit, come!	13
Cry 'Freedom!'	4
From God goes forth	28
From many grains	19
Good news to the poor	5
He is not here	24
In the darkness of the garden	25
Jesus meets us	14
Mary, blessed teenage mother	20
Such a host as none can number	9
The Spirit of God	5
The voice from outside	27
Who would believe	11

THE WITNESSING COMMUNITY

Angels and stars	27
As we walk from pain and sorrow	26
Behold and see	6
Christ bids us seek his face	8
Come, Holy Spirit, come!	13
Come, let us, in this holy place	1
Cry 'Freedom!'	4
From God goes forth	28
From the very depths of darkness	29
Good news to the poor	5
He is not here	24
I do not know the man	15
Jesus meets us	14
Look to the rock	3
Mary, blessed teenage mother	20
Such a host as none can number	9
The Creed	17
The Spirit of God	5
The voice from outside	27
We believe	17
Who would believe	11

THE SUFFERING COMMUNITY

As we walk from pain and sorrow	26
At your feet	30
Behold and see	6
Blest are you O God, Creator	18
Christ bids us seek his face	8
Come, Holy Spirit, come!	13
Cry 'Freedom!'	4
From God goes forth	28
From many grains	19
In the darkness of the garden	25
Into your hands	23
It is complete!	21
Jesus meets us	14
Keep watch and pray	10
Mary, blessed teenage mother	20
O why, my God, have you forsaken me	7
Such a host as none can number	9
The Creed	17
We believe	17
Who would believe	11

THE PILGRIM COMMUNITY

As we walk from pain and sorrow	26
Come, let us, in this holy place	1
Look to the rock	3
Spirit of God	22

CHURCH UNITY

Angels and stars	27
At your feet	30
Cry 'Freedom!'	4
From many grains	19
From the very depths of darkness	29
Glory to God	16
Good news to the poor	5
Hail to the risen Lord	12
Look to the rock	3
Such a host as none can number	9
The Creed	17
The Gloria	16
The voice from outside	27
We believe	17

WORSHIP

INVOCATION AND CALL TO WORSHIP

Come, Holy Spirit, come!	13

Come, let us, in this holy place	1
Glory to God	16
Hail to the risen Lord	12
Jesus meets us	14
Spirit of God	22
Such a host as none can number	9
The Gloria	16
We believe	17

PRAISE AND THANKSGIVING

Blest are you O God, Creator	18
Come, let us, in this holy place	1
Glory to God	16
Hail to the risen Lord	12
Look to the rock	3
Such a host as none can number	9
The Creed	17
The Gloria	16

PENITENCE AND FORGIVENESS

God of the nations	2
I do not know the man	15
In the darkness of the garden	25

INTERCESSION

Come, Holy Spirit, come!	13
Come, let us, in this holy place	1
Cry 'Freedom!'	4
From God goes forth	28
God of the nations	2
Spirit of God	22

HOLY COMMUNION

As we walk from pain and sorrow	26
At your feet	30
Blest are you O God, Creator	18
Christ bids us seek his face	8
Come, Holy Spirit, come!	13
From many grains	19
Glory to God	16
Good news to the poor	5
Hail to the risen Lord	12
Jesus meets us	14
Such a host as none can number	9
The Creed	17

The Gloria	16
The Spirit of God	5
We believe	17

BAPTISM/CONFIRMATION

At your feet	30
Blest are you O God, Creator	18
Come, Holy Spirit, come!	13
Come, let us, in this holy place	1
From many grains	19
Good news to the poor	5
Hail to the risen Lord	12
Into your hands	23
Keep watch and pray	10
Look to the rock	3
Spirit of God	22
Such a host as none can number	9
The Creed	17
The Spirit of God	5
We believe	17

RECEPTION INTO CHURCH MEMBERSHIP
See Baptism/Confirmation

ORDINATION/INDUCTION
See Baptism/Confirmation

ECUMENICAL WORSHIP
See Church Unity

THE CHURCH'S YEAR

ADVENT

Behold and see	6
Christ bids us seek his face	8
From God goes forth	28
Jesus meets us	14
Such a host as none can number	9

CHRISTMAS

Angels and stars	27
Christ bids us seek his face	8
Glory to God	16
Jesus meets us	14

Mary, blessed teenage mother	20
The Gloria	16
The voice from outside	27

LENT

I do not know the man	15
Keep watch and pray	10
Who would believe	11

PASSIONTIDE/GOOD FRIDAY

Behold and see	6
Christ bids us seek his face	8
God of the nations	2
I do not know the man	15
Into your hands	23
It is complete!	21
Keep watch and pray	10
O why, my God, have you forsaken me?	7
Who would believe	11

EASTER

Christ bids us seek his face	8
Cry 'Freedom!'	4
From the very depths of darkness	29
Glory to God	16
He is not here	24
It is complete!	21
Look to the rock	3
Such a host as none can number	9
The Creed	17
The Gloria	16
We believe	17

ASCENSION

Glory to God	16
Hail to the risen Lord	12
Such a host as none can number	9
The Creed	17
The Gloria	16
We believe	17

PENTECOST

Come, Holy Spirit, come!	13
Good news to the poor	5
Spirit of God	22
The Creed	17
The Spirit of God	5
We believe	17

HARVEST (OF THE KINGDOM)

At your feet	30
Behold and see	6
Blest are you O God, Creator	18
Come, let us, in this holy place	1
Cry 'Freedom!'	4
From many grains	19
From the very depths of darkness	29
Good news to the poor	5
It is complete!	21
Such a host as none can number	9
The Spirit of God	5

REMEMBRANCE SUNDAY

As we walk from pain and sorrow	26
Come, let us, in this holy place	1
God of the nations	2
I do not know the man	15
Who would believe	11

Index of Biblical References and Allusions

This index, even more than the others, can only be regarded as a guide. It cannot be exhaustive since many of the themes and images used in the hymns occur very frequently in the Bible.

EXODUS 6:7-9
Spirit of God — 22

DEUTERONOMY 30:19
Spirit of God — 22

ISAIAH 2:1-4
Come, let us, in this holy place — 1

ISAIAH 9:2
From God goes forth — 28

ISAIAH 42:1-4
Behold and see — 6

ISAIAH 51:1-3
Look to the rock — 3

ISAIAH 51:4
From God goes forth — 28

ISAIAH 53:1-5
Who would believe — 11

AMOS 5:24
It is complete! — 21

MICAH 4:2-4
Come, let us, in this holy place — 1
It is complete! — 21

ZECHARIAH 2:10
From God goes forth — 28

MALACHI 3:1
From God goes forth — 28

MATTHEW 1:1-18
Angels and stars — 27
The voice from outside — 27

MATTHEW 1:18-23
Mary, blessed teenage mother — 20
From God goes forth — 28

MATTHEW 2:1-18
Angels and stars — 27
The voice from outside — 27

MATTHEW 3:1-10
Angels and stars — 27
The voice from outside — 27

MATTHEW 11:5
From God goes forth — 28

MATTHEW 11:18
Angels and stars — 27
The voice from outside — 27

MATTHEW 12:22-32
Keep watch and pray — 10

MATTHEW 16:22-23
Keep watch and pray — 10

MATTHEW 17:1-13
Keep watch and pray — 10

MATTHEW 21:1-13
Keep watch and pray — 10

MATTHEW 21:32
Angels and stars — 27
The voice from outside — 27

MATTHEW 25:31-46
Christ bids us seek his face — 8
From God goes forth — 28
Jesus meets us — 14

MATTHEW 26:36-46
In the darkness of the garden — 25

MATTHEW 26:69-75
I do not know the man — 15

MATTHEW 27:46
O why, my God, have you forsaken me? — 7

MATTHEW 28:6
He is not here — 24

MARK 1:1-8
Angels and stars — 27
The voice from outside — 27

MARK 7:24-30
   Angels and stars   27
    The voice from outside   27

MARK 10:32-45
   Keep watch and pray   10

MARK 14:32-42
   In the darkness of the garden   25

MARK 14:66-72
   I do not know the man   15

MARK 15:34
   O why, my God, have you forsaken me?   7

MARK 16:6
   He is not here   24

LUKE 1:26-35
   Mary, blessed teenage mother   20

LUKE 1:46-55
   Mary, blessed teenage mother   20

LUKE 2:8-20
   Angels and stars   27
    The voice from outside   27

LUKE 2:14
   From God goes forth   28

LUKE 4:1-13
   Keep watch and pray   10

LUKE 4:18
    Good news to the poor   5
   Such a host an none can number   9
   The Spirit of God   5

LUKE 7:12
   Jesus meets us   14

LUKE 7:33
   Angels and stars   27
    The voice from outside   27

LUKE 16:21
   Jesus meets us   14

LUKE 22:40-46
   In the darkness of the garden   25

LUKE 22:54-62
   I do not know the man   15

LUKE 23:46
   Into your hands   23

LUKE 24:5
   He is not here   24

LUKE 24:13-35
   As we walk from pain and sorrow   26
   He is not here   24

LUKE 24:50-53
   Hail to the risen Lord   12

JOHN 1:19-28
   Angels and stars   27
    The voice from outside   27

JOHN 2:1-10
   Christ bids us seek his face   8
   Jesus meets us   14

JOHN 5:2
   Jesus meets us   14

JOHN 8:32
   From God goes forth   28

JOHN 10:9
   Jesus meets us   14

JOHN 10:10
   Jesus meets us   14

JOHN 18:25-27
   I do not know the man   15

JOHN 19:1-37
   Keep watch and pray   10
   It is complete!   21

JOHN 20:17
   From the very depths of darkness   29

ACTS 1:9-11
   Hail to the risen Lord   12

ACTS 2:1-3
   Spirit of God   22

ACTS 3:1-10
   Jesus meets us   14

ACTS 3:2
   Jesus meets us   14

ACTS 3:10
   Jesus meets us   14

ACTS 10			*The voice from outside*	27
Angels and stars	27		I CORINTHIANS 12:8-11	
The voice from outside	27		Come, Holy Spirit, come!	13
ACTS 10:17			I CORINTHIANS 13	
Jesus meets us	14		Come, Holy Spirit, come!	13
ACTS 11:1-18			REVELATION 7:9-17	
Angels and stars	27		Such a host as none can number	9

Index of Biblical Characters

ABRAHAM
    Look to the rock   3

CORNELIUS
    Angels and stars   27
    The voice from outside   27

HEROD
    Angels and stars   27
    The voice from outside   27

JACOB
    Come, let us, in this holy place   1

JAMES AND JOHN (SONS OF ZEBEDEE)
    In the darkness of the garden   25
    Keep watch and pray   10

JESUS
(See Index of Uses; God: The Son)

JOHN THE BAPTIST
    Angels and stars   27
    The voice from outside   27

MARY MAGDALENE
    From the very depths of darkness   29

MARY (MOTHER OF JESUS) (See Index of Uses)

PETER
    Angels and stars   27
    I do not know the man   15
    Keep watch and pray   10
    The voice from outside   27

PHARISEES
    Keep watch and pray   10

SHEPHERDS
    Angels and stars   27
    The voice from outside   27

SUFFERING SERVANT
    Behold and see   6
    Who would believe   11

SYRO-PHOENICIAN WOMAN
    Angels and stars   27
    The voice from outside   27

WISE MEN
    Angels and stars   27
    The voice from outside   27

Music from Kevin Mayhew

Favourite Anthem Book 4

A collection of twenty-five anthems for SATB. The accompaniments to the older anthems have been newly arranged and set out for organ, making it much easier for the organist to produce more effective results. Arranged by Harrison Oxley.

Almighty Lord and God of love	N. Leighton	*Now the God of peace*	G. H. Knight
Ascension Carol	Dutch melody	*O for the wings of a dove*	F. Mendelssohn
Ascribe unto the Lord	John Travers	*O gladsome light*	Harrison Oxley
Call to remembrance	Richard Farrant	*O God, our help in ages past*	Walford Davies
Cantate Domino	G. O. Pitoni	*O Lord, increase my faith*	Henry Loosemore
Expectans Expectavi	Charles Wood	*O sweet and blessed country*	Gustav Holst
God be in my head	Walford Davies	*O worship the Lord*	John Travers
God omnipotent reigneth	Charles Wood	*Panis angelicus*	César Franck
Greater love hath no man	John Ireland	*Rejoice to God*	A. Gumpelzhaimer
Hear my prayer	F. Mendelssohn	*Round me falls the night*	Adam Drese
How beauteous are their feet	C. V. Stanford	*Tell it out amongst the heathen*	John Travers
Jesu, dulcis memoria	T. L. de Victoria	*This joyful Eastertide*	Harrison Oxley
My soul, there is a country	C. H. H. Parry		

1425308

Favourite Anthem Book 5

The latest title in this famous series with thirty more unison and two-part anthems. Edited and arranged by Richard Lloyd.

A Christmas Song	H. Statham	*My Jesus, O what weight of woe*	J. S. Bach
An earthly tree	William Byrd	*O leave me not, my everlasting God*	J. S. Bach
Ave Maria	Flor Peeters	*O turn away mine eyes*	William Boyce
Bist du bei mir	J. S. Bach	*Panis angelicus*	M. A. Charpentier
Come, let us this day	J. S. Bach	*Quid retribuam Domino*	G. de Lioncourt
Drop, drop, slow tears	Frank Bridge	*Rejoice in the Lord alway*	Henry G. Ley
God grant us peace	B. Wickham	*Salve, Regina*	M. A. Charpentier
Hear my prayer, O God	Thomas Norris	*The sun shall be no more thy light*	Maurice Greene
I lie down with God	Donald Swann	*The sorrows of my heart*	William Boyce
It is a thing most wonderful	John Ireland	*The Call*	R. V. Williams
I will lay me down in peace	Maurice Greene	*The Virgin's Slumber Song*	Max Reger
I will magnify thee, O Lord	Joseph Corfe	*Thou, O God, art praised in Sion*	Joseph Corfe
Jesus Christ the apple tree	Derek Holman	*Why art thou so vexed, oh my soul?*	C. H. Trevor
Jesu, the very thought of thee	C. S. Lang		
Let all the world in every corner sing	C. S. Lang		
Litany	Franz Schubert		
Lowly, laid in a manger	John Ireland		

1425309

Kevin Mayhew Ltd Rattlesden Bury St Edmunds Suffolk IP30 0SZ
Phone 0449 737978 Fax 0449 737834